COOL CARS

FORD MUSTANG SHELBY GT500

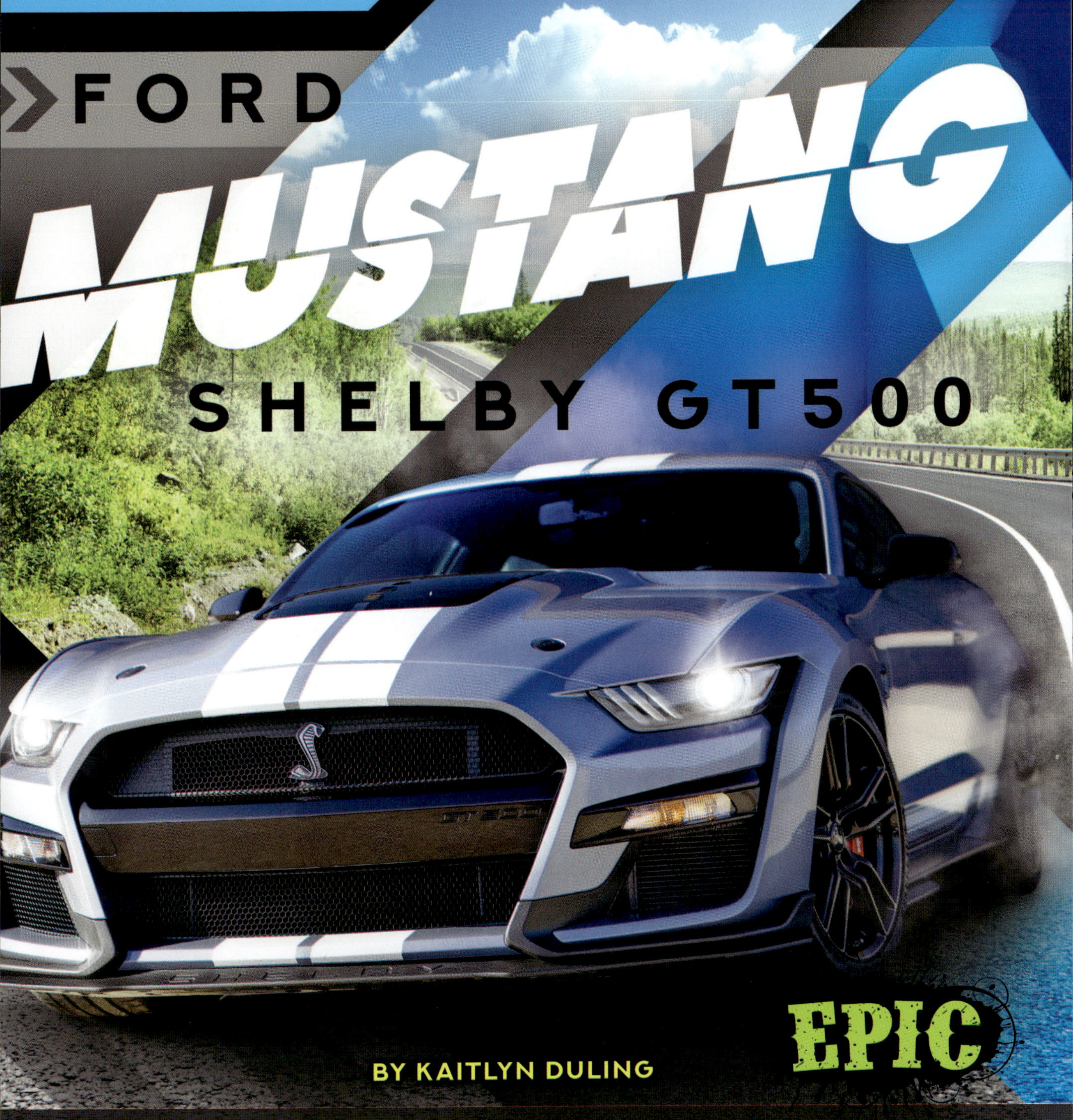

EPIC

BY KAITLYN DULING

BELLWETHER MEDIA ››› MINNEAPOLIS, MN

EPIC

EPIC BOOKS are no ordinary books. They burst with intense action, high-speed heroics, and shadows of the unknown. Are you ready for an Epic adventure?

This edition first published in 2025 by Bellwether Media, Inc.

Library of Congress Cataloging-in-Publication Data

Names: Duling, Kaitlyn, author. Title: Ford Mustang Shelby GT500 / by Kaitlyn Duling.
Description: Minneapolis, MN : Bellwether Media, Inc., 2025. | Series: Epic. Cool cars | Includes bibliographical references and index. | Audience: Ages 7-12 | Audience: Grades 2-3 |
Summary: "Engaging images accompany information about the Ford Mustang Shelby GT500. The combination of high-interest subject matter and light text is intended for students in grades 2 through 7"-- Provided by publisher.
Identifiers: LCCN 2024002290 (print) | LCCN 2024002291 (ebook) | ISBN 9798893040548 (library binding) | ISBN 9781644879948 (ebook)
Subjects: LCSH: Mustang automobile--Juvenile literature. | Shelby, Carroll, 1923-2012--Juvenile literature. | Muscle cars--United States--Juvenile literature.
Classification: LCC TL215.M8 D875 2025 (print) | LCC TL215.M8 (ebook) | DDC 629.222/2--dc23/eng/20240205
LC record available at https://lccn.loc.gov/2024002290
LC ebook record available at https://lccn.loc.gov/2024002291

Editor: Rachael Barnes Designer: Jeffrey Kollock

Printed in the United States of America, North Mankato, MN.

TABLE OF CONTENTS

MIGHTY MUSTANG

The muscle cars cross the finish line.
The mighty Ford Mustang Shelby GT500 wins!

ALL ABOUT THE SHELBY GT500

1913 FORD ASSEMBLY LINE

The Ford Motor Company started in 1903. It was the first to build cars on **assembly lines**.

Ford began making Mustangs in the 1960s. They have powerful engines. They are small and stylish cars.

1960S MUSTANG

Ford started working with Shelby American to build Mustang **variants**. The Shelby GT500 was first sold in 1967. It was only made until 1970.

The next Shelby GT500 rolled off the line in 2007. It was made until 2014.

SHELBY SNAKE

Fans look for a metal cobra on Mustangs. It shows which cars are made with parts from the Shelby American company.

METAL COBRA

1968 GT500 CONVERTIBLE

SHELBY GT500 BASICS

YEAR FIRST MADE	1967
COST	starts around $80,795
HOW MANY MADE	around 13,000 from 2020 to 2022

FEATURES

grille

spoiler

racing stripes

FORD FACTORY IN FLAT ROCK, MICHIGAN

INSIDE THE FACTORY

The latest Shelby GT500 ran from 2020 to 2022. It was built in Flat Rock, Michigan.

It is one of the fastest and most powerful Mustangs!

WHERE WAS IT MADE?

PARTS OF THE SHELBY GT500

The Shelby GT500 has a **V8 engine**. It can reach 60 miles (97 kilometers) per hour in 3.4 seconds!

The engine sends power to the rear wheels.

ENGINE SPECS

SUPERCHARGED V8 ENGINE

TOP SPEED	180 miles (290 kilometers) per hour
0-60 TIME	3.4 seconds
HORSEPOWER	760 hp

KING OF THE ROAD

In 2022, Ford released the GT500KR. Only 225 were made. It is known as the King of the Road!

The Shelby GT500's front **grille** takes in air. This air passes by the engine to cool it. Then it exits through a **hood vent**.

A **spoiler** helps the car grip the road at high speeds.

The Shelby GT500 has six drive modes. Normal and Slippery modes are meant for daily driving.

SIZE CHART

Some modes are used for racing. Sport, Track, and Drag Strip modes help drivers win!

Some Shelby GT500s are **customized**. Many buyers add racing stripes. Others choose the **Heritage Edition**. It looks like the 1967 GT500.

WHY THE LINES?

Racing stripes have been added to cars since the 1950s. Fans could spot their favorite race cars on a crowded track.

HERITAGE EDITION

TRACK PACK REAR

Buyers choose the Track Pack to make their car lighter and faster. These cars have no rear seats!

THE SHELBY GT500'S FUTURE

Ford stopped building the Mustang Shelby GT500 in 2022. It is expected to return.

Ford is testing a new **convertible** Shelby GT500. Fans hope to see this muscle car soon!

GLOSSARY

assembly lines—connected lines of workers and machines that are used to put things together

convertible—a car with a folding or soft roof

customized—made to personal order

grille—a set of bars that cover an opening on the front of a car; the grille allows air to enter and exit the engine.

Heritage Edition—a type of car made to honor a special car in the company's history; heritage edition cars often have the same name and look as the original car.

hood vent—an opening in a car's hood that allows air to enter and exit

muscle cars—American-made two-door sports cars with powerful engines

spoiler—a part on the back of a car that helps a car grip the road

V8 engine—an engine with 8 cylinders arranged in the shape of a "V"

variants—models that are closely related to but notably different from base models

TO LEARN MORE

AT THE LIBRARY

Duling, Kaitlyn. *Ford GT.* Minneapolis, Minn.: Bellwether Media, 2023.

Emminizer, Theresa. *Mustangs.* Buffalo, N.Y.: Enslow Publishing, 2023.

James, Ryan. *Muscle Cars.* Coral Springs, Fla.: Seahorse Publishing, 2022.

ON THE WEB

FACTSURFER

Factsurfer.com gives you a safe, fun way to find more information.

1. Go to www.factsurfer.com.
2. Enter "Ford Mustang Shelby GT500" into the search box and click 🔍.
3. Select your book cover to see a list of related content.

INDEX

The images in this book are reproduced through the courtesy of: Ford, front cover, pp. 3, 4, 5, 6, 9 (isolated, spoiler, stripes, and grille), 10 (main and inset), 11, 12, 13, 14 (main and hood), 15, 16 (main and width), 17 (main and length), 18, 19 (main and seats), 20, 21; The Image Engine, p. 8; Johnnie Rik, p. 7; Birgit Reitz-Hofmann, p. 8 (metal cobra).